AF255800

Notes for a Postlude

Notes for a Postlude

poems

JEREMIAH WEBSTER

Foreword by J. P. O'Connor

RESOURCE *Publications* • Eugene, Oregon

NOTES FOR A POSTLUDE
Poems

Resource Publications
An Imprint of Wipf and Stock Publishers
199 W. 8th Ave., Suite 3
Eugene, OR 97401

www.wipfandstock.com

PAPERBACK ISBN: 978-1-6667-4387-6
HARDCOVER ISBN: 978-1-6667-4388-3
EBOOK ISBN: 978-1-6667-4389-0

VERSION NUMBER 09/05/23

For Liam and Madelyn . . . and for orphaned believers
everywhere.

The wolf shall dwell with the lamb,
and the leopard shall lie down with the young goat,
and the calf and the lion and the fattened calf together;
and a little child shall lead them.

ISAIAH 11:6

And yet, when the Son of Man comes,
will he find faith on earth?

—LUKE 18:8

Fourteen poems in this collection originally appeared in the following print and online journals:

Crab Creek Review: *Other Space*

Mockingbird: *Witness 1, 2, 3, 4* / *Middle Age* / *The Weeds of Eden* / *Tulips* / *Extinction Event* / *On the Nature of My Premature Soul and Its Capacity to Know God in the Incubator of Twenty First Century America*

North American Anglican: *The Collar*

Relief: *Gospel* / *Letter to My Grandson (Who is Probably a Cyborg)* / *The Solemn Sea*

Contents

Foreword

Mary's Song and the God of Luke[1]

From the humble body of Mary bellows some of the most commanding words in the Gospel of Luke:

> My soul magnifies the Lord, and my spirit rejoices in God my Savior, for he has looked with favor on the lowly state of his servant. Surely from now on all generations will call me blessed, for the Mighty One has done great things for me, and holy is his name; indeed, his mercy is for those who fear him from generation to generation. He has shown strength with his arm; he has scattered the proud in the imagination of their hearts. He has brought down the powerful from their thrones and lifted up the lowly; he has filled the hungry with good things and sent the rich away empty. He has come to the aid of his child Israel, in remembrance of his mercy, according to the promise he made to our ancestors, to Abraham and to his descendants forever (Luke 1:46b–55; trans. NRSVue).

Preceding these words in Luke's opening chapter, the reader learns that this story may upend the very firmament of the present social order. An angel by the name of Gabriel abruptly appears before Mary in her private residence in the small town of Galilee: "Greetings, favored one," the angel announces. Mary is beside

---

1 Portions of this material are adapted with permission from O'Connor, *The Last Shall Be First: The Judgment of God according to the Gospel of Mark* (Waco: Baylor University Press, forthcoming).

herself. As Henry Ossawa Tanner's extraordinary, late 19th century depiction of the scene illustrates, Mary appears uneasy and unassuming before this angelic beam of light.[2] Gabriel repeats his honorific greetings: "you have found favor (*charin*) from God." In v. 32, Mary is told that the son she will bear will be "great" (*megas*) and given the title "Son of the Most High." This "great" king originates in the lowliest of places. The Son of the Most High is not born in royal courts it would seem but in the "lowliest of [God's] servants" (v. 48). Mary cannot keep this monumental news a secret. "With speed" she runs to Elizabeth's house to share what has taken place. In the joyous company of her kin, Mary bursts into a song of praise. "My soul magnifies the Lord, and my spirit rejoices in God my Savior."

Then, her song of devotion takes an unmistakably political turn.

Mary, from the small town of Galilee, who carries within her body a soon and coming king, declares that God, the "powerful one" (*ho dunatos*) who has done "great things" (*megala*) for her, will topple the mighty with the child in her womb. We are told that kings are stripped of their thrones and the rich have lost all their material wealth. In a breathtaking reversal, it is the "lowly," the "hungry," and "his child" who have been raised up to take their place.

From the outset of Luke's Gospel, God takes the "weak things of the world to shame the strong" (1 Cor 1:27). As Brian Blount has forcefully demonstrated, such a task belongs to Luke's "primary ethical agenda." Blount expounds, "Empowering the oppressed and humbling the mighty is more than a call for spiritual repentance; it is a bid for social repentance that will have concrete historical impact if it is lived out in the way that Jesus… demanded."[3] The Lukan impulse to present a Jesus who empowers those on the margins of society may be found throughout his

2 https://philamuseum.org/collection/object/104384.

3 Brian K. Blount, *Then the Whisper Put on Flesh: New Testament Ethics in an African American Context* (Nashville: Abingdon Press, 2001), 89.

Gospel (4:18; 6:20; 7:22; 14:13, 21; 16:20, 22).[4] Yet, unlike Mark's more cataclysmic, apocalyptic ethics, Luke invites his readers to take up the "daily" task of following Jesus (9:23; cf. Mark 8:34).[5] Luke challenges his readers to implement this way of life as a new standard that poses a grave threat to the Roman political apparatus. The reversal of insiders and outsiders partially submerged in Matthew and Mark is now made plain in Luke. One might consider here the "Sermon on the Plain" (Luke 6:20–26) in which the Matthean beatitudes are no longer transcendental categories (see "poor in spirit" or "hunger and thirst for righteousness" in Matt 5:3–12) but concretized people within history (see "the poor" or "the hungry"). Mary's song, in this way, operates as a blueprint that guides the reader's journey through the Gospel.[6] God intends to upend rigid social and cultural boundaries for the liberation of those on the margins and for the humbling of those at the top. We tap our foot to the rhythm of Mary's tune throughout the story, leading up to its definitive expression in Jesus's final hours. Some have argued that Luke's passion scene portrays Jesus as the ideal, self-controlled man—with the bravado of Sylvester Stallone.[7] A close reading, however, reveals the opposite in places. Jesus is in great agony leading up to his final days (22:44) and, at the pinnacle of his suffering, he extends forgiveness and mercy to his enemies instead of vindictive retaliation (23:34, 43). Furthermore, his bodily torment is more readily identified with the life of an enslaved person than with a king.[8] In the words of Brittany Wilson, "Jesus fails to protect the boundaries of his body on every front and is ultimately nailed to a cross."[9] According to Luke, the

---

4 Blount, *Then the Whisper*, 81.

5 Blount, *Then the Whisper*, 83.

6 Blount, *Then the Whisper*, 87.

7 See criticism of this position in Brittany Wilson, *Unmanly Men: Refigurations of Masculinity in Luke-Acts* (New York: Oxford University Press, 2015), 191.

8 Wilson, *Unmanly Men*, 229–30.

9 Wilson, *Unmanly Men*, 234.

unfolding, cosmic plan of divine redemption manifests in the meek and vulnerable bodies in our world.

A THEOLOGICAL RECKONING

Jeremiah Webster's stunning collection of poems sings in the same tune as Luke the Evangelist. In "Evangelical," Webster writes, "I never found the verse / where power is the currency / of heaven's beatitude." To which Mary sings, "He has brought down the powerful from their thrones." One can visualize Webster's priest in "The Collar" seeking the same reversal as he is pulled down "in among the poor." Luke's Gospel marches in a similar fashion, yanking down all who wear the so-called collar of discipleship. *Notes for a Postlude* disrupts the calcitrant Left/Right binary of American politics, points the imagination toward the revelators of the natural world (see "Witness I-IV"), and echoes the beatitude-economy of Jesus's Sermon on the Mount. Hardly the passive observer of our societal discontent, the speaker in Webster's poetry is at turns crestfallen, big-hearted, hopeful, and knowingly complicit in the crisis. Rather than observe the destruction from a safe cloister, the poet weeps among the ruins.

Notes for a Postlude aims to rectify with a Lukan spirit our very definition for power and its proper theological allocation. "Notes for a Postlude," for instance, leaves us with the haunting surprise of the corpse of "this pale American Christ" and only picks up steam from there. "Witness" considers the power of a solitary, whispered prayer in comparison to the domineering presence of a military drone. Luke, sometimes called "the evangelist of prayer," demonstrates considerable interest in a Jesus who prays (see Luke 3:21; 5:16; 6:12; 9:18, 28–29; 10:21–22; 11:1–2; 22:32, 39–46; 23:34, 46).[10] Instead of turning to the powers of this world in times of turmoil, Luke's Jesus turns to God, the source of all power, and he invites his followers to do the same. Webster's "Evangelical" exposes how

10 See Geir O. Holmås, *Prayer and Vindication in Luke-Acts: The Theme of Prayer within the Context of the Legitimating and Edifying Objective of the Lukan Narrative*, LNTS 433 (New York: T & T Clark/Bloomsbury, 2011).

the sacrosanct liturgies of the American church are at odds with the teachings of Jesus. Those who justify violence on the grounds of "self-defense," worship a God who did not defend himself even when violently seized (Luke 22:54). Similarly, "Trump Tongue™" counts the cost of one's solidarity with a "virulent tongue" and the incalculable harm such words wreak upon the ones we love. One here is reminded of the words of Jesus to do good to those who seek out our destruction (Luke 6:27–30). How can we turn our cheeks if our mouths are full of hatred?

The insurgence of Christian nationalism in America has sounded the alarm for those committed to the teachings of the crucified Nazarene. Properly defined, Christian nationalism "is a cultural framework—a collection of myths, traditions, symbols, narratives, and value systems—that idealizes and advocates a fusion of Christianity with American civic life."[11] On the more extreme end of its expressions, sociologists make note that the animus for those aligned with this particular cultural narrative is the desire for power.[12] In other words, the teachings of Jesus regarding love and mercy are often secondary to the need for maintaining social and cultural dominance. In many ways, the January 6th insurrection has become an indelible mark upon the Christian nationalist zeitgeist.[13] The intermingling of participants in the Jericho March with those who would later take siege of the U.S. Capitol Building

11 Andrew L. Whitehead and Samuel L. Perry, *Taking America Back for God: Christian Nationalism in the United States* (Oxford University Press, 2020), 10.

12 See Whitehead and Perry's chapter entitled, "Power," in *Taking America Back for God*, 55–87.

13 See Emma Green's "A Christian Insurrection" *The Atlantic*, January 8, 2021. https://www.theatlantic.com/politics/archive/2021/01/evangelicals-catholics-jericho-march-capitol/617591/. The image of the erected gallows outside the Capitol contains scribbled religious jargon in writing, including "In God We Trust." see the upload by user Tm on Jan 10 2021: https://upload.wikimedia.org/wikipedia/commons/a/a6/2021_storming_of_the_United_States_Capitol_DSC09417-2_%2850814530472%29.jpg. For insight regarding the theological animus for members of the Jan. 6th assault, see Nancy Duff, "Apocalyptic Ethics, End-Time Christians, and the Storming of the US Capitol," *SCE* 34 (2021): 467–81.

serves as a startling parable with which Webster's work attempts to reckon. Reports inform us that Christian participants bubbled over with laudatory shouts at both the rallying cry, "shout if you love Jesus," as well as "shout if you love Trump."[14] Webster's poetry holds up a mirror for the American church, inviting us to revisit our finite creatureliness before "the God of us all." In parabolic fashion, Webster confronts us in places like "The Weeds of Eden," to ask with whom we have aligned—to the mythic tradition of the "present evil age" (Gal 1:4) or to the cross of our crucified Lord.

The following introduction aims to situate Webster's work within the biblical and theological narratives of the early church. These pages serve as a mere addendum to what amounts to a deeply enriching theological exposé. Our own reckoning with the God of Abraham must begin with a theme prevalent in the poems that follow—human finitude in the face of the end. "In a land with no sabbath / where utility is king / it's time to bury the dead / with a solemn offering." Webster's work invites us to consider the fragility of our own existence in the presence of an all-powerful God. "Body Count" adopts a striking realism in the wake of COVID-19; "guided tours of those refrigerated trucks" recounts the apocalyptic moment when the nation viewed droves of the deceased in trucks on live television. In a slightly different tone, "Father" depicts Webster daydreaming about life's potential calamities as his children inquire innocently about the volition of backyard plants. Have we lost such innocence in our grown-up pursuits and our inundation with perennial disasters? "Middle Age," in a similar manner, draws attention to the ever-present imposition of mortality as we age. What power do we have to enact change in this world? Likewise, the biblical authors wrote with a sense for the end. The Scriptures wrestle with our creatureliness and the end we all face (see Gen 2:7; Eccl 3:20–21; Ps 104; Job 40). The biblical authors also write theologically, that is, they arrange their literary compositions God-ward. The sobering effect of the biblical witness from Genesis to Revelation is a naked confrontation between humans and God. "What is a man that you are mindful of him?" the

14 Green, "A Christian Insurrection."

Psalmist inquires. As we learn in the parables of Jesus, those of us committed to the way of the cross must ask, in the end, where we stand in relation to God. Are we among the sheep or the goats? The wheat or the tares? Have we taken the narrow road or opted for the broad one instead? The Scriptures also teach that our bodies of dust, molded from the mud of the earth, must give an account before the Creator (Rom 14:10; 2 Cor 5:10). In what follows, I offer three images of creaturely accountablity from the Scriptures, which I hope bolster the robust theological reckoning with which Webster calls us toward in *Notes for a Postlude*.

THE GOD OF DANIEL

In the book of Daniel, some argue that the role of the "wise teachers" (1:4; 11:32–35; 12:3, 10) was to safeguard the people of Israel against the onslaught of reforms by Antiochus IV in the early Hellenistic period.[15] According to 1 Maccabees, King Antiochus' rise to power held great possibilities for those under his care. By building a gymnasium in Jerusalem and integrating the cultural norms of the surrounding nations, many were enthralled with their new-found king (1 Macc 1:10–15). Antiochus' power, however, quickly turned violent. He defiled the holy Temple of YHWH, outlawed Jewish customs, and killed anyone who stood in his way (1 Macc 1:29–64). The author of 1 Maccabees tells us that "many even from Israel gladly adopted his religion" (1:43; trans. NRSVue). Their reasons for doing so are unclear. Perhaps some within Israel sought to avoid Antiochus' decree of death upon those who resisted his reforms; others may have been enticed by his mesmerizing promises of power. Regardless, the author describes a persecuted minority who resisted and remained faithful to the covenant of YHWH despite the mounting pressure of cultural assimilation (1:62–64). In a similar move, Daniel 11:31–32 offers a window into a comparable social ethos:

15 Dating Daniel is a rather complex issue; see Carol A. Newsom with Brennan Breed, *Daniel: A Commentary*, OTL (Louisville: Westminster John Knox Press, 2014), 8–12, 216.

> Forces sent by him shall occupy and profane the temple
> and fortress. They shall abolish the regular burnt offering
> and set up the desolating sacrilege. He will flatter with
> smooth words those who violate the covenant, but the
> people who are loyal to their God shall stand firm and
> take action (trans. NRSVue).

If one compares the analogue background of 1 Maccabees to Daniel, then much of Daniel's writing serves to strengthen a community under inexplicable duress (see Dan 10:19; 12:3, 13) as well as to promise future vengeance upon those who seek their harm (10:20–21). According to Daniel, those within Israel who have compromised with the ruling authorities undergo a process of refinement (Dan 11:35). Furthermore, this group of "wise ones" is clearly differentiated from the "wicked" who do not understand (12:10).[16] The prevalent theme within Daniel 7–12 is of a future judgment against the Seleucid empire for the sake of empowering people on the fringes of society, or as Daniel has it, "the many" (11:33–34). Reminiscent of Mary's Song (Luke 1:46b–55) the God of Daniel seeks to protect God's children and to bring low those who abuse their power.

The God of Mark

A similar impulse may be found in the New Testament. In the brief parable of "The Lamp and the Measure" in the Gospel of Mark (4:21–25), those possessing a "measure" (*metron*) may expect more to be given, while those who have nothing may expect more to be taken away. Losing that which one holds dear recalls Jesus's invitation earlier in the Gospel to forsake one's own life as the paradigmatic configuration for discipleship (Mark 8:34–38).[17]

---

16 There is debate surrounding the social class of Daniel's *maśkîlîm*. For more, see Anathea Portier-Young, *Apocalypse Against Empire: Theologies of Resistance in Early Judaism* (Grand Rapids: Eerdmans, 2010), 232–33.

17 For the case that final judgment is the context here, see Brian Han Gregg, *The Historical Jesus and the Final Judgment Sayings in Q*, WUNT 2.207 (Tübingen: Mohr Siebeck, 2006), 259–68.

Frustratingly, however, Mark does not clearly spell out who will do the giving and who will do the taking nor who will be the recipient of either the gaining or the losing. John Calvin reads this parable as an overt threat to those who abuse their power: "The wickedness of the Papists is therefore intolerable."[18] According to Calvin, anyone endowed by God with authority remains liable for the mistreatment of those under their care. Perhaps Calvin is right here, but who is the one taking away these elevated positions of great power? Satan is one possibility: the mischievous one who steals the seed along the path (Mark 4:4, 14). A divine passive also seems quite plausible.[19] Of the Synoptics, Mark alone contains the parable of the seed that grows secretly situated right after (4:26–29). The curious parable serves as an intertext to interpret the one before. The second parable recounts a farmer who sows his seed but then does nothing to nurture its growth. By some miracle, the seeds begin to sprout. Flabbergasted, the farmer "knows not how" (4:27) but the seed has grown "automatically." By reading these two parables side-by-side one can see that God and God's power are located at the forefront of truculent social realities. Some believe that Mark's audience, similar to Daniel's, belongs to a persecuted minority within the Roman empire.[20] To those who suffer, the God of Mark declares that God will come and make things right (12:9; 13:13, 24–27). For the farmers entrusted with the task of seed-sowing who have grown weary of their work, they must recall that God is the one who gives and takes away. Our task is simply to pay attention.

18 John Calvin, *Commentary on a Harmony of the Evangelists: Matthew, Mark, and Luke*, trans. William Pringle, Calvin's Commentaries (repr. Grand Rapids: Baker Book House, 1996), 271–74, here 271.

19 See C. Clifton Black, *Mark*, ANTC (Nashville: Abingdom Press, 2011), 124–26.

20 See David Rhoads, *The Challenge of Diversity: The Witness of Paul and the Gospels* (Minneapolis: Fortress Press, 1989), 76.

THE GOD OF REVELATION

Lastly, in the book of Revelation, John declares that God will judge each according to their deeds including all who have misused their power in opposition to God's people (see Rev 6:10; 11:18; 14:7; 16:5, 7; 18:8, 10, 20; 19:2, 11; 20:12–13). The Apocalypse associates the "great dragon" with "the Devil and Satan" who exist to deceive humanity and to wreak havoc upon the earth (12:7–17). Most scholars acknowledge that John intends a veiled criticism of Rome with his metaphor here. In other words, the enemy, as one sees in the book of Daniel or 1 Maccabees, is the political order of dominance. Revelation's dragon deceives universally: the entire world worships him (13:3–4). The misconduct of this evil creature is unequivocally described as blasphemous, authoritarian, and a declaration of war against the saints (13:5–8). The end for such evil is forthcoming and final (14:10–11; 17:11, 16). Rome's defeat provokes great sorrow among those complicit in her systems of wealth. Kings and merchants alike weep as the "great city" is "thrown down" never to rise again (18:11, 21). Among the chief offenses listed here, "living in luxury" (*strēniaō*) appears twice (18:7, 9). For those who revel in their wealth to the determent of the widow: "your judgment has come" (18:7–10). God condemns Rome for a multitude of sins: harming God's people (11:7; 12:10, 17; 16:6; 17:6), haughtily assuming the role of God (13:4–5, 12), and inciting the people to act in ways contrary to God's law (14:8). In this final image of divine accountability, God intends to protect God's children and to bring low the Roman elite including all those entangled in Rome's regime.

"THE GOD OF US ALL"

In each of the three examples above, we see a stiff warning against political powers and those who wield unruly authority alongside of them. The biblical witness does not mince words here: the dragons and beasts who misuse power in this age will have a high price to pay in the age to come (see Mark 9:42–50). We also learn that God cares dearly for God's children. The reason some of the children of God might be reprimanded, as one finds in the case of the "wise ones" in Daniel, is for the possibility of refinement (Dan 12:10). Bringing low the proud opens the door for repentance. Mark's Gospel teaches us that God intends to protect God's children. In the twin parables examined above, God brings about the harvest though the farmer knows not how. God is the principal actor who takes away from those who have pawned off the way of God for the ways of the world (see Mark 4:18–19; 8:34–38; 12:17).

Notes for a Postlude is a welcome course correction. The poems survey the broken liturgies of our post-truth moment and offer a compelling alternative. This alternative eschews rigid dogmatism and laissez faire morality. This alternative is suspicious of demagogues and empty religious rhetoric. This alternative leads us to a place where Christians perceive God's active presence among the poor like Dorothy Day, receive revelation from the natural world like St. Francis of Assisi, and find "Jesus in *Poetics*" (See "On the Nature . . .") like St. Thomas Aquinas. The poems exhibit a robust "catholic" imagination that sees God's active presence in the world, despite the present darkness and the evils done in God's name. Ultimately, the apocalyptic register of the verse is hopeful. With a nod to Milton's *Paradise Lost*, Webster ends his collection with "The Solemn Sea," a poem that intimates the final redemption of our broken estate – that all indeed shall be well – that God shall be "all in all" (1 Cor 15:28).

The God of us all
sustains the depths of the sea,

hangs His wings in satisfaction over the world
He has made.

The God of us all
consumes creation's diminished return,
the nature study war grave vessel love-wreck
of our solitary way.

The God of us all
is the same God

some believe
walks upon waves,

broods over waters,
until the solemn sea is wine dark

once more.

J. P. O'CONNOR

NOTES FOR A POSTLUDE

It was Luther who taught us
and his minions of reform
how to silence the mystics
and make the Gospel conform.

Converse with pagan and muse
was left in the God-hid wood
for bards to find such riches
where early Chistians once stood.

In a land with no sabbath
where utility is king
it's time to bury the dead
with a solemn offering.

Gaze upon the corpse's face
before the slate stone is set.
Recite the beatitudes
pastors told us to forget.

Offer hymns of renegade
like a pious athiest.
Pray God, do not resurrect
this pale American Christ.

WITNESS / 1

More majestic than any drone
is the eagle in its fixed flight
until the static of its repose
is shattered by a single
mouse, an answered
prayer.

LITERACY

"I don't read,"
a student informs me. First day.
Couldn't this wait, I think
(one never says) until after
the Pequod's maelstrom? In the middle
of some terminal passage from Dryden, perhaps?
Before Winston's "Do it to Julia!" Section 3. Chapter 5.
My vote for reliable horror in prose.

No. This is preemptive.
Pre-Cambrian in its disregard
for what a future of books might hold.
Pre-syllabus even, which merely ticks me off.
So I think about reading
(the class is staring now)
in a world where the prerogatives
of perfect teeth, health care,
copulation, and consumerism
eclipse the fact that we all die anyway.
And I wonder, save for books,
who can warn us of the innate catastrophe?
Who can rise from the ether and say,

I understand.
I read you.

MIDDLE AGE

inaugurates a sudden compulsion
to support my local NPR station,
introduce more fiber into the diet,
lose enthusiasm for pop culture,
Google-search "frequent urination
prostate health" and worry
that I metamorphosized
into a constipated crank
during one of Ovid's midnight
TP raids upon the psyche.

Middle age asks that I parent
in an empire of illusion, see
my children safely home
through a pandemic wood
full of conspiratorial carnivores,
wolves in women's clothing,
baby-faced zealots sporting
legal assault rifles.

Middle age is the via media
of novice and notable,
as liable to streak in public
as laze about poolside.
Middle age is the trickster's
creaky crawlspace, the art
of saving face, that bedeviled
in-between season where the hero
of the D&D campaign

faces the dreaded
colonoscopy.

Middle age says "No"
with ease, is dismissed
as outmoded, past-prime,
a has-been, dim
as mortality cuts in
to write whole chapters
(*Misgivings, Maladies*)
into the waning
biography.

Middle age is as bardic
and barbaric as the Middle Ages:
Zarathustra of the Mountain
gone mad with tenure, disaffected,
cynical, save for a late term dose
of grace-sprung wonder.

Middle age is the place where ego
yields its whaling harpoon, ceases
all strife, the place where love
is mistaken for losing,
the place where even God
gives His life away.

BODY COUNT

We need to know where the beloved
Covid dead are stored for burial.

We need it out in the open,
masked or no, vaxxed
or no, not on a spreadsheet,
not massaged with math, or managed
like the inconvenience of hornets on holiday.

We need guided tours of those refrigerated trucks,
shovels for every able-bodied citizen
to dig graves on the manicured lawns of City Hall.
Call it community service.
Call it quality time with the family.
Call it the charisma of a corpse
who interrupts normalcy
again and again and again.

Perhaps then all the smug snark
will dissolve like a contrarian moon,
the exception reflex go slack
like a line with no fish,
and we will know
something of Priam's tears,
when he wept for sister-stranger
among perennial dead.

THE WEEDS OF EDEN

sprout from the blood of Cain,
coil hooked vines around verdant
trunks, green stalks, skirt
extraction with leaves that mimic
indigene.

The weeds of Eden talk secession,
sanctimony, hijack water
with tapping tendrils,
are impervious
to fertilizers designed
to weed out hatred
of vegetable neighbors.

The weeds of Eden are naked
and have no shame,
look upon the wilt of death
and laugh, are pliable,
brittle, savage,
a syrupy sick.

See how the gardener weeps,
returns to the shade with a book
when he cannot distinguish
choice crop
from counterfeit.

CROW FUNERAL

After another mass shooting
in America (and before
the next one), crows
become our native priests.

Hear the polished stones
of their beaks
cry out for a fallen comrade.
Watch them circle the corpse
in feathered robes of onyx.
Listen as they recall
how cousin Raven,
God's mortician,
taught Cain how to bury
a murdered brother.

WITNESS / 2

The world sleeps
as I walk to my monk's cell.
Two raccoons, fat off the city
Gates built, growl from an autumnal
tree, dare me to abandon
the pressed flannel,
the briefcase—scrap in the leaves
like Sid Vicious offspring
until I'm dead
to the envy
of gold.

TRUMP TONGUE™

I'd prefer the domestic
danger of a loaded gun
over a virulent tongue
that feels up my wife,
extorts futures from my children,
and laps water with the dog.

True, the sight of a naked tongue
is comedy gold, winning fun
for ratings, the bloviation
of its boasts aligned
with every Sunday School
vice.

I watch it slither
off the television,
across the living
room floor, breed
monosyllabic
misfits, confuse
tantrum with cogent
thought.

People I love act
like it isn't there, re-enact
past abuses, make tribal
excuses, and revel
in the gonzo of our now.

When the tongue catches fire,
ignites the drapes, the couch,
I search in vain for brother Rousseau
to extinguish the disaster.

As flames consume the house,
friends and relatives envy-post
how the light looks like
success, a star
gone supernova.

EVANGELICAL

Evangel, meaning "gospel,"
from the Anglo Saxon, *godspell*,
from the Old French, *évangile*,
from the Greek, *euangelion*,
to bring good news.

I watch them wield guns
like sacred relics, recycle the myth
of faceless homeland invaders,
claim self-defense as divine edict
from their crucified American god,
and read Herod's elementary school slaughter
as a pretext to stash high-capacity magazines
in the bedside drawers of Gideon.

They tell me abortion is immoral
only to elect a Caligula,
deploy activist judges,
and embitter the secular imagination
to the necessary enchantment
of God become flesh become fetus become son
in the womb of an unwed teenage mother.

Money conspires on their mouths,
a metric of success more invested
in the principal of the Zodiac
than the poverty of a deprived
Jewish carpenter,
and I never found the verse
where power is the currency

of heaven's beatitude, never
discovered the apocryphal text
that sanctions Manifest Destiny, never
read the epistle where Paul commends the church
at Ephesus for "owning the libs."

In the story I learned from Mr. Hamilton,
my sixth grade Sunday School teacher,
paraplegic, less disabled than most,
every tongue, tribe, and nation
joins a feast, a repertoire for every palette,
and division fades like celebrity
trivia and the dates of wars
amid those dinner plates
as the Host dishes up an end
to hunger and hatred
for good.

GOSPEL

Do stories fail, negate
themselves, seek haven
with huckster, heathen,
hang their promise from the rafters
like David Foster Wallace: the progress
of enlightened centuries?

Is the world content with a world
where the bones of nymphs, gnomes
preserved in enviable revelry, are never found,
where leviathan has no dominion,
where flowers are only caught,
crushed in the machinery,
where Leda receives no recompense,
where Frodo is left for dead?

Here I am, past forty, in good health,
educated beyond what is healthy for a man,
deferential (though discontent)
in the ossified Cartesian mold,
seeking word beyond death,
word without end:

procreative torso

    starfish limb

       dormant seed

          empty tomb.

SANCTUARY

Along the riverbank of a spent youth
I find the preternatural pool
where the servants of Pisces
rise in a regalia of scales,
ministers of slant-light to a weary
body (now waist deep) in the dark
sermon of the current's mercy.

I submerge myself to silence
the voices of our political
bereavement, voices that rant
and never read, voices in league
with Calvin's gospel of a cloistered
elect, succored in a grim-gated Elysium.

The lack of oxygen, an embryonic
estate, a silence to rival Simeon,
is preferable to the airways above
where "thought leaders"
conceive a dominion
with civil war
for our children.

With suicide never stocked
in the arsenal of grace,
I ask aquatic priests to recite
the incantation, *Kyrie Eleison*,
wizard-like, until the body
politic dissolves like a dandelion

on the benevolent ceiling
of the pool's abyss.

ENEMY LOVE

MATTHEW 18:21-22

Strange to see the heart's tally
increasingly occupied
with professing believers,
the too-busy-on-Sundays,
who beckon apocalypse
with John Darby
and a Capitol riot.

Seven is the perfect odd
number (like the Trinity).
It eschews easy pairing
for sudden community.
But the math confounds the soul
like an impervious curse
and there is deep communal
betrayal as Jesus fans
offer antichrist talking
points to defend church abuse
and the next theocracy.

Lord, give me an expansive
hate-defying panoply,
beyond slight ability,
an ark-haven envelope
to not just endure, but love
my nuclear enemy.

ON THE NATURE OF MY PREMATURE SOUL AND ITS CAPACITY TO KNOW GOD IN THE INCUBATOR OF TWENTY FIRST CENTURY AMERICA

If I die before I am due,
rack it up to reliable
American optimism,
that preternatural instinct
to find beauty in the shadows
stolen from Japanese bodies,
goodness in fossil fuel trade routes
once locked in a sea of glacier,
and truth in the incredulous
mimicry of the megachurch.

Let the judgment be merciful
on a soul cradled in comfort,
a soul pastored in capital,
a soul that forgets it's a soul
in a gilded market of grift.

If I die before I am due,
rack it up to reliable
American theology,
that ahistorical instinct
to revise the angel's herald
from "all people" to "our people,"
to write sermons of amnesia,
Sola Reforma, as rebel

witnesses disrupt the zeitgeist
to find Jesus in *Poetics*.

Let the judgment be merciful
on a soul created of dust
and divinity, complicit
in the brokenness God endures
to make all things radiant right.

I eat wild blueberries
along an abandoned logging road
just off Highway 2 in the spirited
Cascades. I go off trail to climb
the forested ridge for a view
of Frog Mountain, a view
of the black bear who grazes
in the valley below, a view
where I am trespasser,
blueberry bandit,
surveyor of harmony
lost.

ENDGAME

It's telling that Gatsby
can't leave Earth fast enough,
that the highest view
a billion dollars can buy
is the stoic void
of vapid space.

Was he relieved to find no oxygen
for the *least of these*, no threat
of regulation, taxes to evade,
or litigious god in that elite
atmosphere?

Whatever crossed his mind
(like a so-much-winning comet)
during the four minutes
of weightlessness,
we the grounded
can only lose.

And as the capsule returned to Earth,
as inevitable as Icarus,
was he grateful to catch a glimpse
of the Ganges,
or was the fall merely occasion
to plan another jaunt
(just like this one)
into oblivion?

PRODIGAL

I was just fine
until I read that the Earth,
a mobile sphere, spins
nineteen miles per second,
67,000 miles per hour,
in a flight path susceptible
to solar flares, rogue asteroids,
and aliens (I hope).

This resigns the race
to perpetual travel, imposed
wanderlust, a coaster even the dead
continue to ride in absentia.

I coddle angst
in my depression room
until God keys the lock,
barges in, tears open
the shutters, throws
up the sash.

"Get up!
Orbit my Sun.
Ride the star cradle
like a celestial halfpipe.
Get on with it.
Even if you choose
to stand."

KLEOS

(Greek: **ΚΛΕΟΣ** */ renown / glory)*

Married to the St. Francis
of Whitman County, you minister
to the birds in a bathrobe,
even when your feet are too swollen
to walk, and the stove sighs in winter
for want of Douglas fir,
and the asthma stifles
your song.

You know each one by name

Junco
 Sparrow
  Goldfinch

Nuthatch
 Chickadee
  Towhee

in a world inclined to make you

Invalid
 Reclusive
  Anonymous.

You make a name
among the birds, pray

with the seasons, take wing
in the four-chambered
cathedral hidden
in the avian heart.

JULY 4, 2023

With the same original
energy as Walt Whitman,
the girl composes her first
lament, Rachel's companion,
turns off the screen long enough
to join a choir of haunted
dryads in a northwest wood
of no upgrade and still time.

With the same original
zeal/geist as Dorothy Day,
the boy chooses to mimic
the witness of the Phoenix,
"Blessed are the poor in spirit,"
as tent cities abolish
the prosperity gospel
he suckled as an infant.

These are the revolutions
I prayed for in Covid Land.
These are the rebel tokens
I stash in drawers to keep faith
as late capitalism
slouches in earnest excess.
Post-Boomer voices that say:

You are more than what you own.

There is life
beyond the (goddamn)
phone.

THE COLLAR

pulls my poverty
in among the poor,
tugs my stiff-necked
affluence toward Jesus
understudies,
breathing icons
I'm priest-inclined
to pass on the street.

ADRIFT / GEDDES

Oil on Board (2011)

As the glass shatters
in the silent vacuum of space
does the cosmonaut renounce
the science that got him there
or is the messenger bird
defying zero gravity
enough to keep faith?

WITNESS / 4

The trees are so green-clad
the raindrops become emeralds
as they fall from a ghost of grey.
The moose, Nature's bohemian,
unemployed, bellows
in a wealth-storm
of wonder.

COURAGE ICARUS, NOW SING

Could I have done any better
above that jade sea,

the moment a pair of waxed wings

made their proud arc
against the gods?

WIFE

Constant inclination
toward hope

beloved who
eclipses

the banal
how do I live

with the scandal
that my death

a cruel vacancy
unbidden denizen

flung from the mind's loft
stamped on the heart's tin

is more indelible
than the designs

of any stranger?

OTHER SPACE

By the glass, by the portal,
by the water's window, by the pane
is my boy, having positioned his stroller
by the aquatic gate, I stand and watch
his eyes mimic the walleye,
his mouth become the bass mouth,
his body go still as the scales that hang
in the care of Pisces before us.
He breaks his gaze
to look at me, seeking
assurances I cannot give, the reason
we reside in this space
and not the other.

FATHER

Certain of calamity,
I mustn't let on when my children,

caught in a current of questions,
inquire if plants have volition

or if the rabbit eating clover
in the backyard ever gets lonely.

I mustn't diminish my daughter's ambition
to be a zoologist for animals near

extinction, or my son's earnest promise
to be brave (after Pinocchio)

in the belly of a whale.
I mustn't be said whale

when the news goes grim,
the melody: maelstrom.

I mustn't flail about
as Liam and Madelyn swim

graceful
beside me.

TULIPS

Don't touch the tulips,

 but they beckon, blush
 in a resin vase, elegant
 even with cut stems divorced
 from Washington soil, and my daughter
 is a blithe Eve in this reenactment
 of the Garden.

Don't touch the tulips,

 but she leans, fingers outstretched,
 tummy-folded along the edge
 of the kitchen table, for a petal
 the variable of sherbet.

Don't touch the tulips,

 and the petal faints
 on contact, falls
 to the counter, beyond
 Daddy repair, now accessible
 in death as my daughter
 looks over at me with eyes
 past innocence:

  You did this with your grave
  command, your prohibition
  of beauty noumenal,
  your lack of faith
  in thy kingdom come.

LETTER TO MY GRANDSON
(WHO IS PROBABLY A CYBORG)

They tell me you have no use for the eyes nature gave you,
or the feet I called "miracle" on your birthday.
They tell me identity is an algorithm,
that you got a once-terminal cancer and lived, twice,
and that your mind has no use for the technology
of books I saved for you on shelves.
They tell me death eludes you, or you it,
and that you refused a trip to the Space Needle
after a tour in virtual reality.
They tell me the Internet is your beloved now,
that you said Mt. Rainier was "unreal"
the day it erupted for good.

I pray you know
grace abides,
meaning *The Lord*,
meaning *no upgrade necessary*,
in some region
of the synthetic organ
that is your heart.

EXTINCTION EVENT

Mrs. Melwood was adamant
that our children would never see
America's patriot bird,
the bald eagle: blotted and botched
from our collective memory.

She spoke with an authority
hard earned by years of primary
school instruction, her furrowed brows
a fatigued witness in repose,
certain of the bird's destiny.

So we sat at our fourth grade desks
and drew preemptive depictions
of the last eagle in crayon,
the last eagle in acrylic,
the last eagle with a mohawk,
the last eagle benediction.

In a dispensation of doom,
how could I forecast the delight
of my children decades later
as a murder of northwest crows
is disbanded by the lightning
of a lone bald eagle in flight?

THE SOLEMN SEA

I.

Given over to unreal industries,
it burns incandescent.
Fish scales float on the surface like cinders.
Pale fish, eyes no longer sea nymph
enchanted, hang in a dead current.
A whale carcass, bones in columns, white chapel,
feeds a legion of anglerfish,
breeds teeth where there is no light.

To plumb such depths takes a word.
To plumb such depths means curiosity
beyond soil: willing ships that sail
inexorably to where Charybdis only
devours, and the children of Phlebas
are dead, and sirens approve
in pools of green slumber.

The solemn sea is no longer wine dark.

II.

She reads books Nobody
reads, *Philosophia Ichthyologica*,
as light (not from but through) the window warms half of her body.
Even in a study her books are quaint, kitsch in their commitment
to dust. Paper houses the world.
Twenty-six letters in residence.
The knowing seam, marginalia (in ink)
adorns the questing permanence of a hardback.
She reads in possession,
possessed by dead oracles,
their voices so faint
no decibel
suffices.

And this also has been one of the dark places of the earth.[1]

What is the source of light?
Of darkness?

The solemn sea is no longer wine dark.

1. Conrad: *Heart of Darkness*

III.

Washed ashore, the Berserker
chews the top of his shield,
readies himself for
weapon-weather
sword-gambit
as the Queen clutches
her ornate throne on the sands of Lewis.

Further up the beach,
a Knight and Bishop of another hue
ready arms, offer prayers to Odin,
mourn their comrade the Rook
swallowed whole by a mackerel
in the deep North Sea.

Faceless Pawns
regain their footing
only to have a trio of waves drag
their squat bodies back out into the depths,
expendable.

Their King observes
the scene in mild
stupefaction, calls
for absent attendants,
inspects his sword for blemish,
and recalls his drunken stupor
during the festival of Walpurgis.

The armies find formation,
face off, as Máni adds
this maritime raid
to his obligation of miracles
to illuminate.

No blood-dimmed tide here.
Only the chipping of ivory
in miniature is heard
above the violent ebb of the sea.

The solemn sea is no longer wine dark.

IV.

Hills green, gold, auburn, and back again
mark our place in a world cut by glacier.

Grain elevators rise like shipwrecks.
A windmill keeps pace
with a wind gust serpentine
from a road of fallen apples
to a rare meeting of trees.

I had not known land to look so much like water,
like waves enchanted by magnetism,
the moon, cratered flood primeval,
fossilized home of brachiopod, trilobite,
where I shoot tin cans with a .22.

It was for me the last wild acreage in America,
subdued by lentil, wheat,
and there below the ridgeline,
graves in congregation
(pre-Gettysburg)
with names that fade
with each passing
harvest.

The solemn sea is no longer wine dark.

V.

Round fog-swept crags the vessel,
seven days east of Nantucket,
imbibes salt water through fissures in the pitch
as waves blast the barnacle hull.

The crew bails in humble
humiliation, knowing the women
back home were right:
the early winter month
too late to make chase.

The captain steers to leeward,
toward the verdant promise
of an uncharted island.
Smoke billows white surrender
as oil in the Hold sloshes about in barrels
fetching twenty eighteen at market.

Marvell, first mate,
prays below deck
as a stowaway eel
(open porthole no doubt),
Eden's serpent,
undulates in water inch-deep.
Cedar beams creak like brittle candies.
The rigging sways, sweats on hooks.

Deliver us from the tempest, O Lord!
Deliver us from the judgment, O Lord!
(Fear overtakes him.)
Deliver us from the eel, O Lord!

Amen . . .
(just in time)
and then the vertical pitch downward.
Enough water for the eel's exit.
Enough water to fill every pair of praying lungs on board.

O fickle prejudice of Poseidon's domain.

Ulysses spared,
Shelley drowned,
the Apostle thrice shipwrecked, saved,
but no accommodation for the crew of Nantucket.
No sudden vantage,
safe harbor,
clime.

The solemn sea is no longer wine dark.

VI.

Even if suicide becomes him,
his book of poems won't match
the critical doting Plath received
at her denouement.

*Why does fierce desire reside
in mediocre intellect?*

He knows every measure
of Mozart's *Requiem*,
a *lacrimosa* he can never
replicate, never
master.

He has memorized poems
of transport, lyric vehicles
that bring words like spells
to strangers, gods that hover
just above the privacy
of his pain.

And over dinner, the way her finger
flicks away a drowning gnat
in her ice water, the pause
that inoculates his letter,
exposes the virgin plea
(dismissed like a dumb waiter),
reinforces the inequity
of love and its beauty.

*Vanity is infinite depth,
infinite possibility.*

The solemn sea is no longer wine dark.

VII.

Who is my sister-brother
if the democracy of the dead
has no vote, if the tears of Priam
are somehow less than a social media feed?

The pagan is preferable.
One thinks.
Never says.

What is life removed
from those who once lived?
Where are mentors if books
(like time machines) no longer
communicate with blinders,
yet blinding clarity all the same?
Better the sinners of history
than the saints of today.

Anyone can throw stones at the dead.

The God of us all
sustains the depths of the sea,

hangs His wings in satisfaction over the world
He has made.

The God of us all
consumes creation's diminished return,
the nature study war grave vessel love-wreck
of our solitary way.

The God of us all
is the same God

some believe
walks upon waves,

broods over waters,
until the solemn sea is wine dark

once more.

About the Authors

J. P. O'CONNOR is the Associate Professor of New Testament at Northwest University. His research has been published widely in academic journals including *The Catholic Biblical Quarterly, The Journal of Biblical Literature, Zeitschrift für die neutestamentliche Wissenschaft, Novum Testamentum,* and *Biblical Interpretation.* His first book is entitled *The Moral Life according to Mark* (Bloomsbury/T&T Clark, 2022) and his second book length project—*The Last Shall Be First: Judgment according to Mark*— is anticipated with Baylor University Press in 2024.

JEREMIAH WEBSTER teaches literature and writing at Northwest University. His poetry has appeared in numerous journals including *North American Review, Beloit Poetry Journal, Crab Creek Review, Dappled Things, Relief, Anglican Theological Review,* and *Mockingbird.* His first poetry collection, *After So Many Fires* (Wiseblood Books), was published in 2018. His first novel, *Follow the Devil / Follow the Light* (Acolyte Press), a fantastique in the tradition of Carroll, Dickens, and Dante, was published in 2023.